THIS JOURNAL BELONGS TO

Copyright 2020 © Kai Reby

All rights reserved. No part of this book may be reproduced without written permission of the copyright owner, except for the use of limited quotations for the purpose of book reviews.

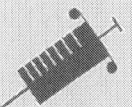 # PET *Vaccinations*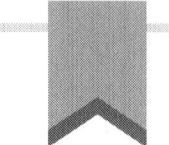

VET
ADDRESS
PHONE
E-MAIL

DATE	AGE	VACCINE	DUE DATE

PET *Profile*

NAME

NICK NAME

BIRTHDAY

ADOPTION DATE

· BASICS ·

BREED

GENDER

EYE COLOUR

COAT COLOUR

UNIQUE MARKINGS

SPAYED / NEUTERED

ID MICRO CHIP#

ALLERGIES

PERSONALITY TRAITS

FAVOURITE TOYS

FAVOURITE TREATS

JANUARY	🐾	☐ ☐	WORMER / FLEA / TICK
FEBRUARY	🐾	☐ ☐	WORMER / FLEA / TICK
MARCH	🐾	☐ ☐	WORMER / FLEA / TICK
APRIL	🐾	☐ ☐	WORMER / FLEA / TICK
MAY	🐾	☐ ☐	WORMER / FLEA / TICK
JUNE	🐾	☐ ☐	WORMER / FLEA / TICK
JULY	🐾	☐ ☐	WORMER / FLEA / TICK
AUGUST	🐾	☐ ☐	WORMER / FLEA / TICK
SEPTEMBER	🐾	☐ ☐	WORMER / FLEA / TICK
OCTOBER	🐾	☐ ☐	WORMER / FLEA / TICK
NOVEMBER	🐾	☐ ☐	WORMER / FLEA / TICK
DECEMBER	🐾	☐ ☐	WORMER / FLEA / TICK

NOTES

 # FIRST *Walk*

AGE	lbs	Oz
8 Weeks		
10 Weeks		
3 Months		
4 Months		
6 Months		
8 Months		
10 Months		
12 Months		

PET *Groomer*

NAME
ADDRESS
PHONE
E-MAIL

FIRST HAIR CUT

PHOTO

PAW Buddies

PET CARE Chart

WEEK COMMENCING _____

	TIME	FOOD/WATER	ACCIDENT	WALK	TRAINING
MON					
TUE					
WED					
THUR					
FRI					
SAT					
SUN					

PROGRESS NOTES

PET CARE Chart

WEEK COMMENCING _____

	TIME	FOOD/WATER	ACCIDENT	WALK	TRAINING
MON					
TUE					
WED					
THUR					
FRI					
SAT					
SUN					

PROGRESS NOTES

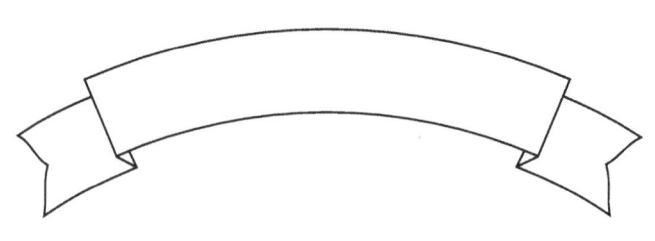

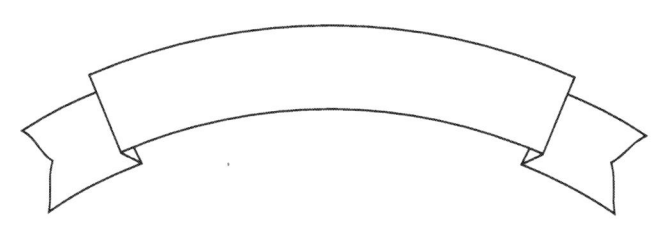

# PET CARE *Chart*

WEEK COMMENCING _____

	TIME	FOOD/WATER	ACCIDENT	WALK	TRAINING
MON					
TUE					
WED					
THUR					
FRI					
SAT					
SUN					

PROGRESS NOTES

PET CARE Chart

WEEK COMMENCING _____

	TIME	FOOD/WATER	ACCIDENT	WALK	TRAINING
MON					
TUE					
WED					
THUR					
FRI					
SAT					
SUN					

PROGRESS NOTES

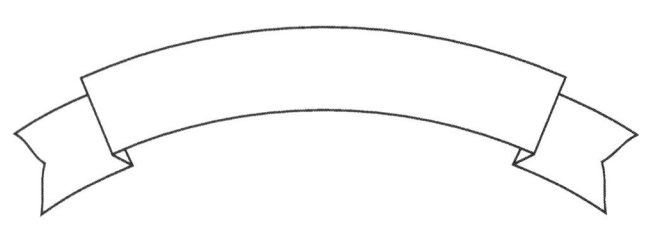

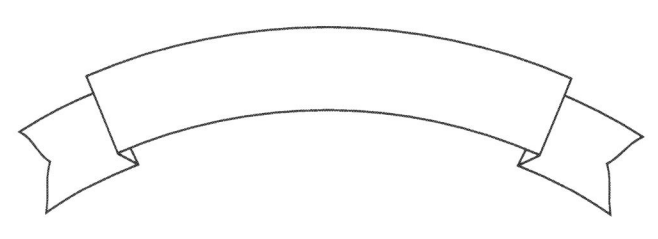

PET CARE Chart

WEEK COMMENCING _____

	TIME	FOOD/WATER	ACCIDENT	WALK	TRAINING
MON					
TUE					
WED					
THUR					
FRI					
SAT					
SUN					

PROGRESS NOTES

PET CARE Chart

WEEK COMMENCING _____

	TIME	FOOD/WATER	ACCIDENT	WALK	TRAINING
MON					
TUE					
WED					
THUR					
FRI					
SAT					
SUN					

PROGRESS NOTES

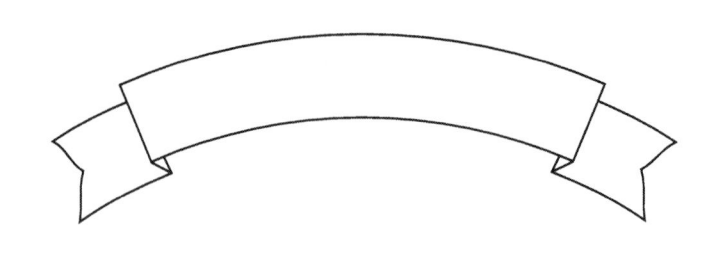

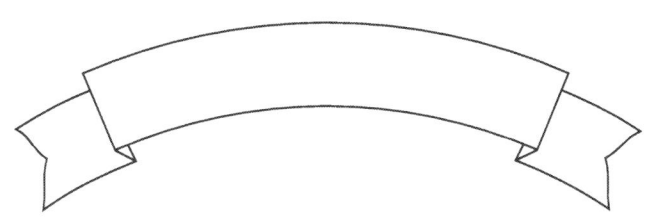

PET CARE *Chart*

WEEK COMMENCING _____

	TIME	FOOD/WATER	ACCIDENT	WALK	TRAINING
MON					
TUE					
WED					
THUR					
FRI					
SAT					
SUN					

PROGRESS NOTES

PET CARE *Chart*

WEEK COMMENCING _____

	TIME	FOOD/WATER	ACCIDENT	WALK	TRAINING
MON					
TUE					
WED					
THUR					
FRI					
SAT					
SUN					

PROGRESS NOTES

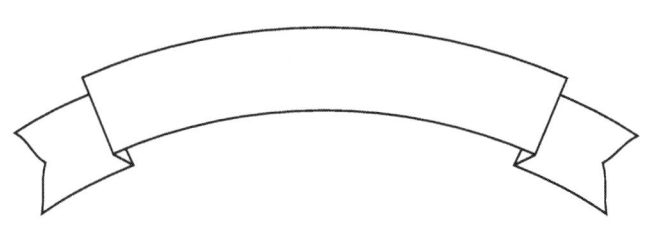

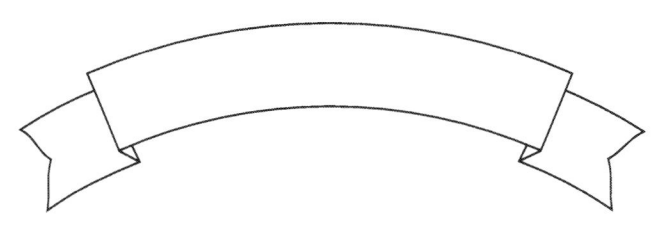

# PET CARE *Chart*

WEEK COMMENCING _____

	TIME	FOOD/WATER	ACCIDENT	WALK	TRAINING
MON					
TUE					
WED					
THUR					
FRI					
SAT					
SUN					

PROGRESS NOTES

PET CARE Chart

WEEK COMMENCING _____

	TIME	FOOD/WATER	ACCIDENT	WALK	TRAINING
MON					
TUE					
WED					
THUR					
FRI					
SAT					
SUN					

PROGRESS NOTES

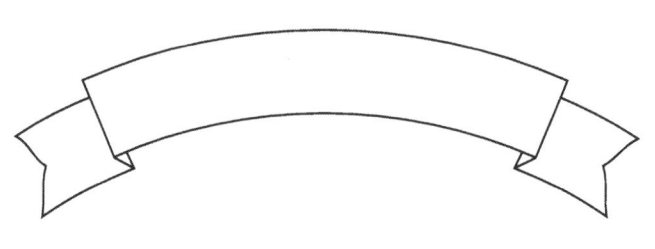

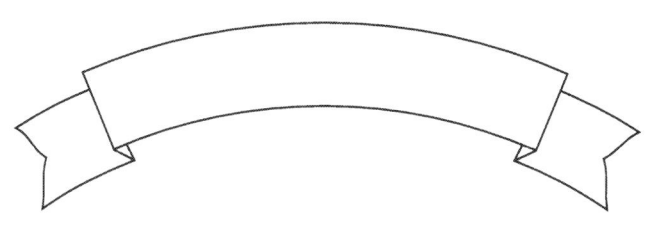

PET CARE *Chart*

WEEK COMMENCING _____

	TIME	FOOD/WATER	ACCIDENT	WALK	TRAINING
MON					
TUE					
WED					
THUR					
FRI					
SAT					
SUN					

PROGRESS NOTES

PET CARE Chart

WEEK COMMENCING _____

	TIME	FOOD/WATER	ACCIDENT	WALK	TRAINING
MON					
TUE					
WED					
THUR					
FRI					
SAT					
SUN					

PROGRESS NOTES

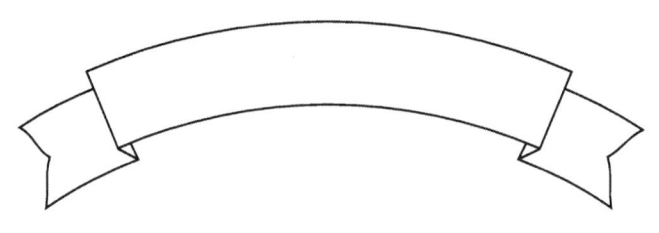

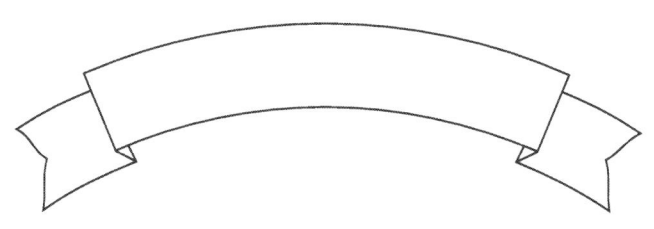

 # PET CARE *Chart*

WEEK COMMENCING _____

	TIME	FOOD/WATER	ACCIDENT	WALK	TRAINING
MON					
TUE					
WED					
THUR					
FRI					
SAT					
SUN					

PROGRESS NOTES

PET CARE Chart

WEEK COMMENCING _____

	TIME	FOOD/WATER	ACCIDENT	WALK	TRAINING
MON					
TUE					
WED					
THUR					
FRI					
SAT					
SUN					

PROGRESS NOTES

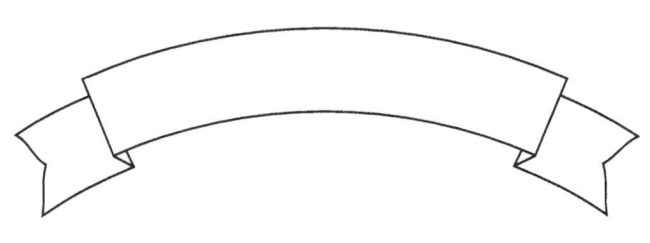

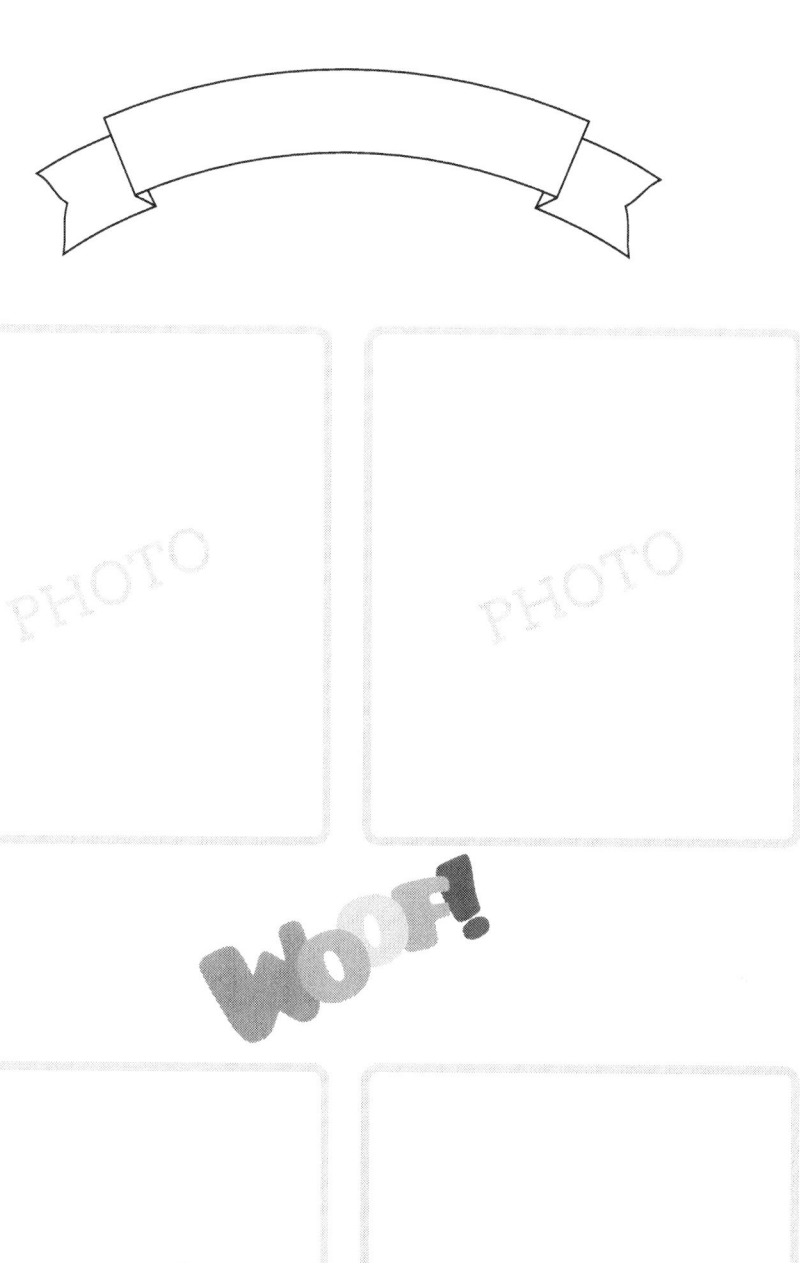

WOOF!

PET CARE Chart

WEEK COMMENCING _____

	TIME	FOOD/WATER	ACCIDENT	WALK	TRAINING
MON					
TUE					
WED					
THUR					
FRI					
SAT					
SUN					

PROGRESS NOTES

PET CARE Chart

WEEK COMMENCING _____

	TIME	FOOD/WATER	ACCIDENT	WALK	TRAINING
MON					
TUE					
WED					
THUR					
FRI					
SAT					
SUN					

PROGRESS NOTES

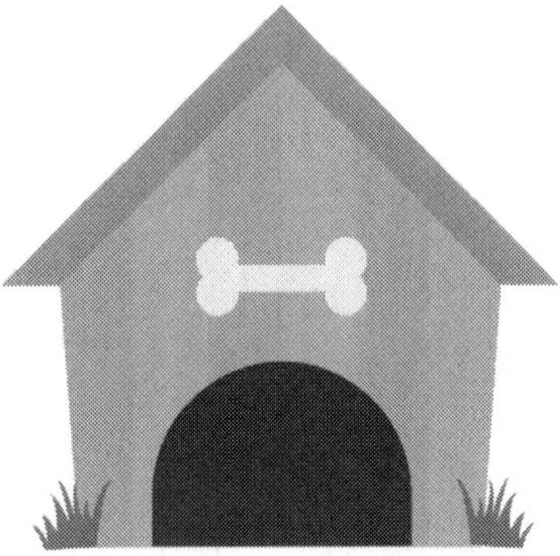

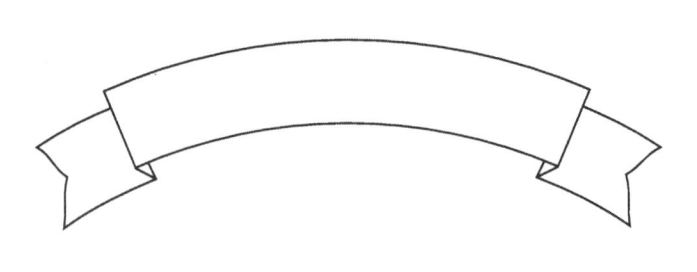

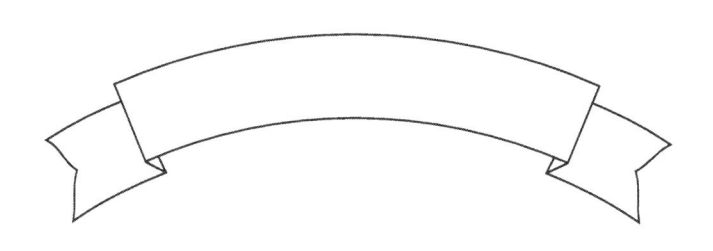

PET CARE Chart

WEEK COMMENCING _____

	TIME	FOOD/WATER	ACCIDENT	WALK	TRAINING
MON					
TUE					
WED					
THUR					
FRI					
SAT					
SUN					

PROGRESS NOTES

PET CARE Chart

WEEK COMMENCING

	TIME	FOOD/WATER	ACCIDENT	WALK	TRAINING
MON					
TUE					
WED					
THUR					
FRI					
SAT					
SUN					

PROGRESS NOTES

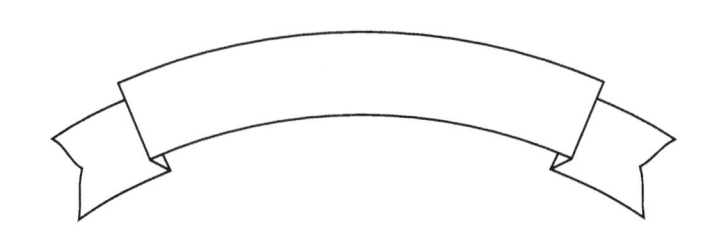

WOOF!

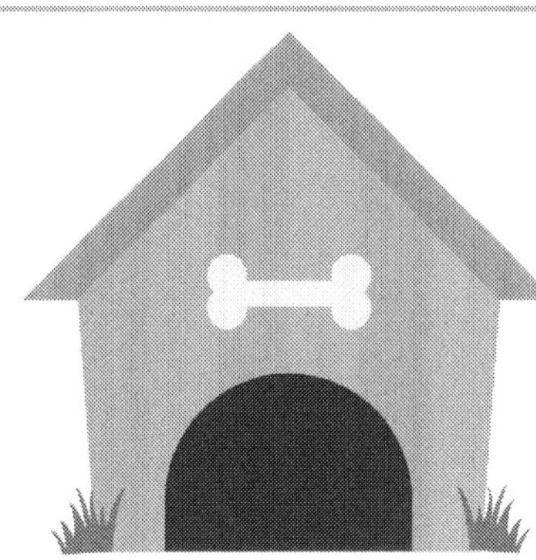

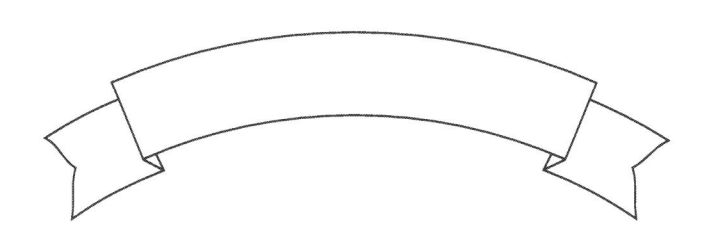

PET CARE Chart

WEEK COMMENCING _____

	TIME	FOOD/WATER	ACCIDENT	WALK	TRAINING
MON					
TUE					
WED					
THUR					
FRI					
SAT					
SUN					

PROGRESS NOTES

PET CARE Chart

WEEK COMMENCING _____

	TIME	FOOD/WATER	ACCIDENT	WALK	TRAINING
MON					
TUE					
WED					
THUR					
FRI					
SAT					
SUN					

PROGRESS NOTES

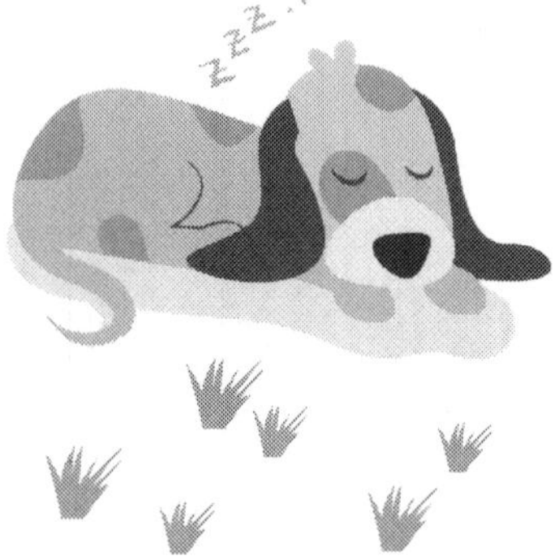

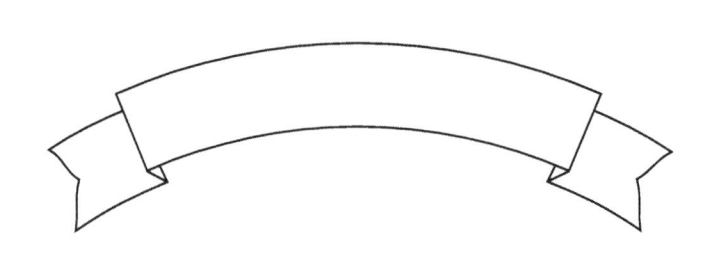

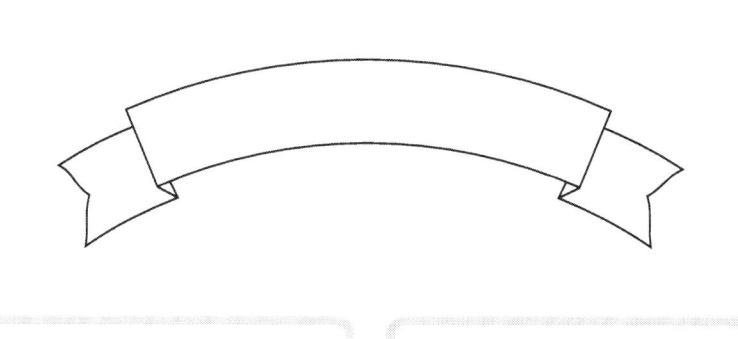

WOOF!

PET CARE *Chart*

WEEK COMMENCING _____

	TIME	FOOD/WATER	ACCIDENT	WALK	TRAINING
MON					
TUE					
WED					
THUR					
FRI					
SAT					
SUN					

PROGRESS NOTES

PET CARE *Chart*

WEEK COMMENCING _____

	TIME	FOOD/WATER	ACCIDENT	WALK	TRAINING
MON					
TUE					
WED					
THUR					
FRI					
SAT					
SUN					

PROGRESS NOTES

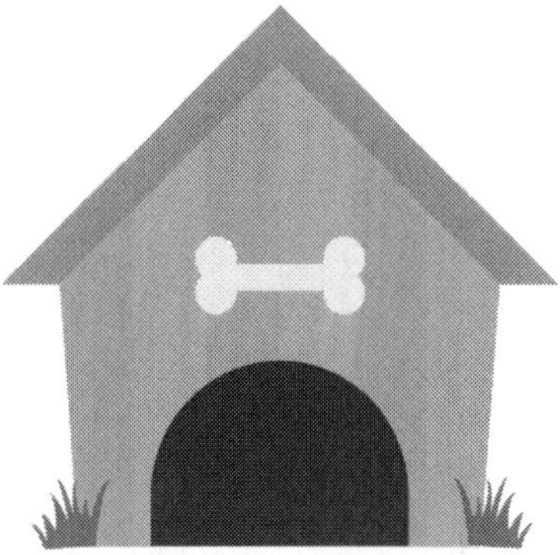

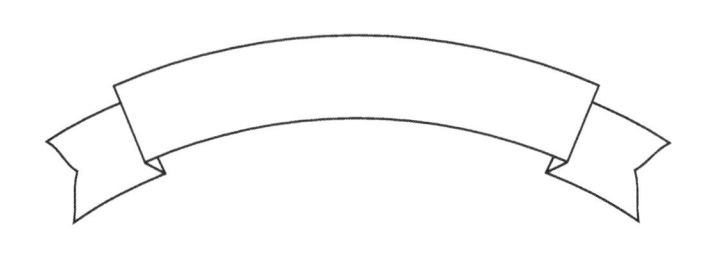

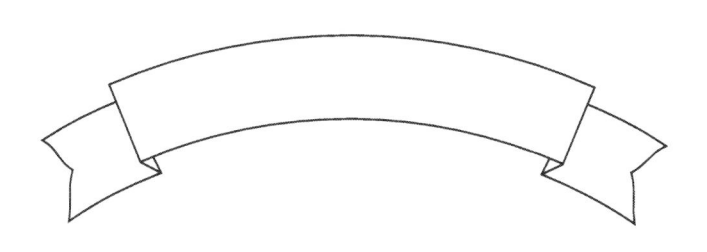

PET CARE *Chart*

WEEK COMMENCING _____

	TIME	FOOD/WATER	ACCIDENT	WALK	TRAINING
MON					
TUE					
WED					
THUR					
FRI					
SAT					
SUN					

PROGRESS NOTES

PET CARE Chart

WEEK COMMENCING _____

	TIME	FOOD/WATER	ACCIDENT	WALK	TRAINING
MON					
TUE					
WED					
THUR					
FRI					
SAT					
SUN					

PROGRESS NOTES

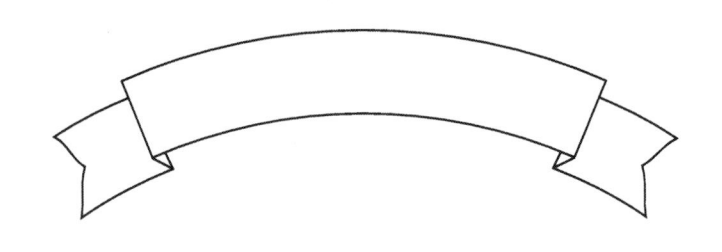

WOOF!

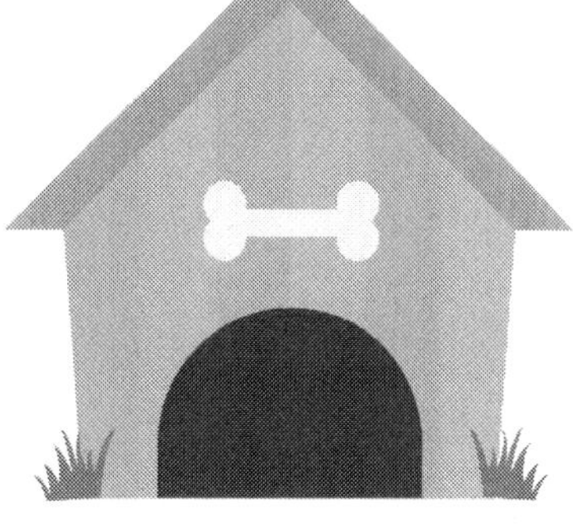

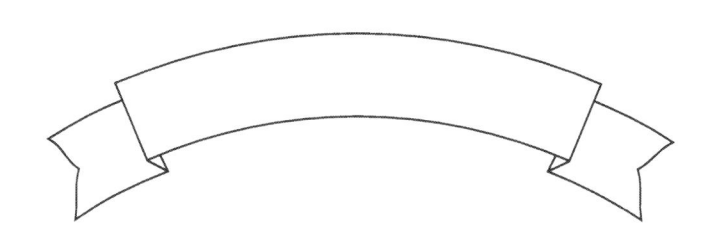

PET CARE Chart

WEEK COMMENCING _____

	TIME	FOOD/WATER	ACCIDENT	WALK	TRAINING
MON					
TUE					
WED					
THUR					
FRI					
SAT					
SUN					

PROGRESS NOTES

PET CARE Chart

WEEK COMMENCING _____

	TIME	FOOD/WATER	ACCIDENT	WALK	TRAINING
MON					
TUE					
WED					
THUR					
FRI					
SAT					
SUN					

PROGRESS NOTES

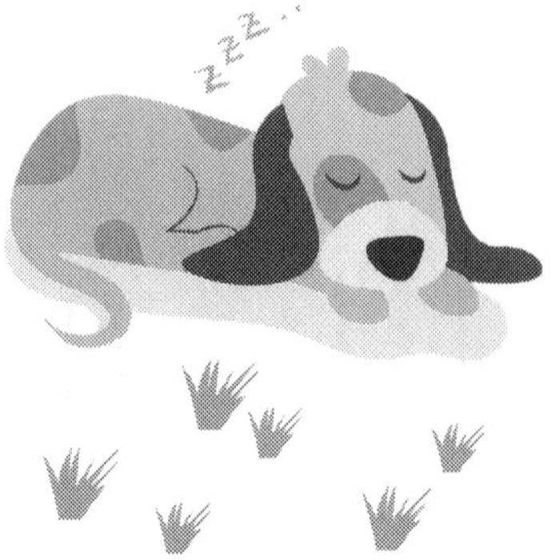

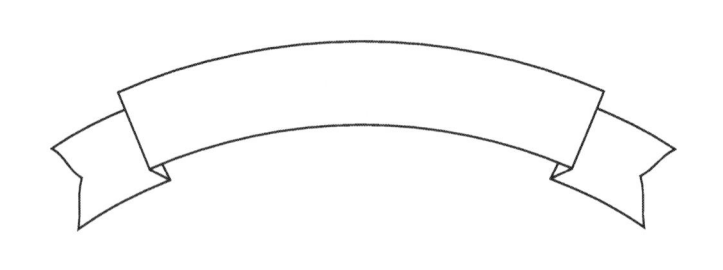

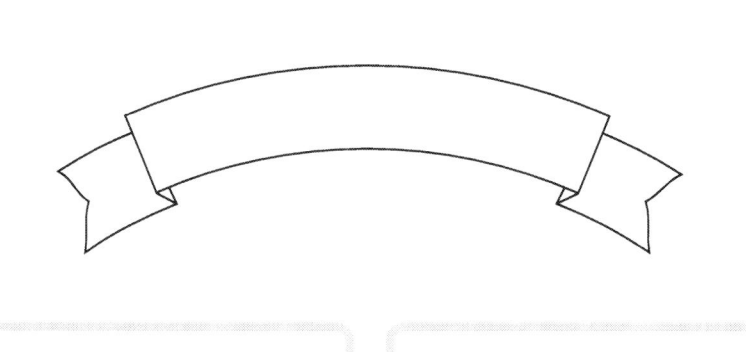

WOOF!

PET CARE *Chart*

WEEK COMMENCING _____

	TIME	FOOD/WATER	ACCIDENT	WALK	TRAINING
MON					
TUE					
WED					
THUR					
FRI					
SAT					
SUN					

PROGRESS NOTES

PET CARE Chart

WEEK COMMENCING _____

	TIME	FOOD/WATER	ACCIDENT	WALK	TRAINING
MON					
TUE					
WED					
THUR					
FRI					
SAT					
SUN					

PROGRESS NOTES

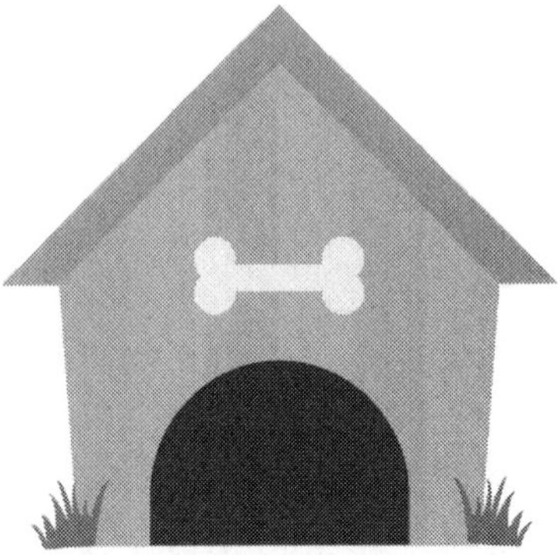

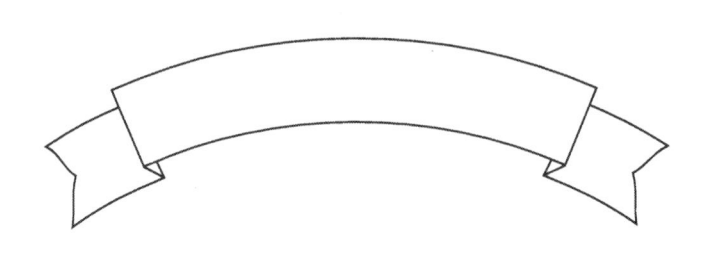

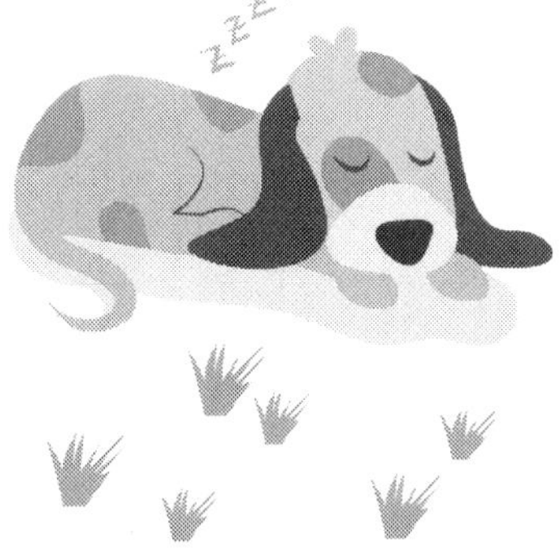

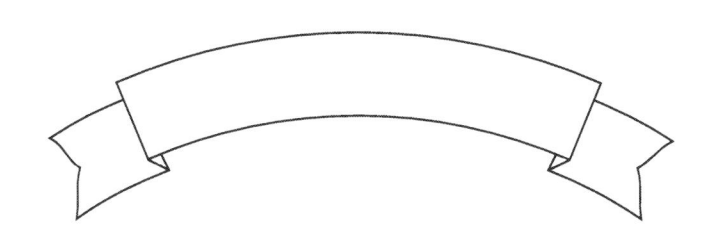

PET CARE *Chart*

WEEK COMMENCING _____

	TIME	FOOD/WATER	ACCIDENT	WALK	TRAINING
MON					
TUE					
WED					
THUR					
FRI					
SAT					
SUN					

PROGRESS NOTES

PET CARE Chart

WEEK COMMENCING _____

	TIME	FOOD/WATER	ACCIDENT	WALK	TRAINING
MON					
TUE					
WED					
THUR					
FRI					
SAT					
SUN					

PROGRESS NOTES

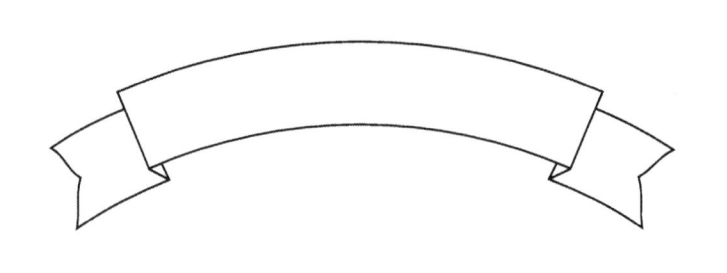

WOOF!

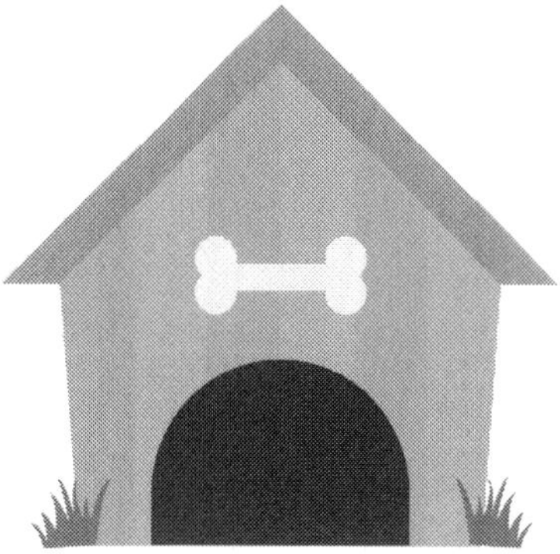

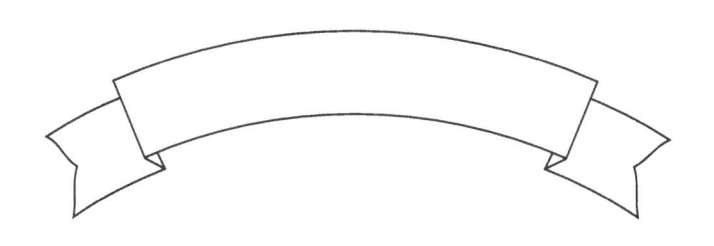

PET CARE *Chart*

WEEK COMMENCING _____

	TIME	FOOD/WATER	ACCIDENT	WALK	TRAINING
MON					
TUE					
WED					
THUR					
FRI					
SAT					
SUN					

PROGRESS NOTES

PET CARE Chart

WEEK COMMENCING

	TIME	FOOD/WATER	ACCIDENT	WALK	TRAINING
MON					
TUE					
WED					
THUR					
FRI					
SAT					
SUN					

PROGRESS NOTES

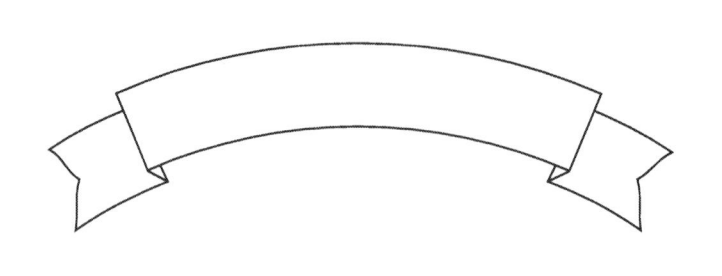

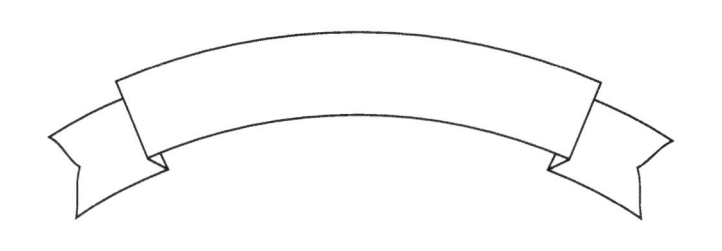

WOOF!

PET CARE *Chart*

WEEK COMMENCING _____

	TIME	FOOD/WATER	ACCIDENT	WALK	TRAINING
MON					
TUE					
WED					
THUR					
FRI					
SAT					
SUN					

PROGRESS NOTES

PET CARE *Chart*

WEEK COMMENCING _____

	TIME	FOOD/WATER	ACCIDENT	WALK	TRAINING
MON					
TUE					
WED					
THUR					
FRI					
SAT					
SUN					

PROGRESS NOTES

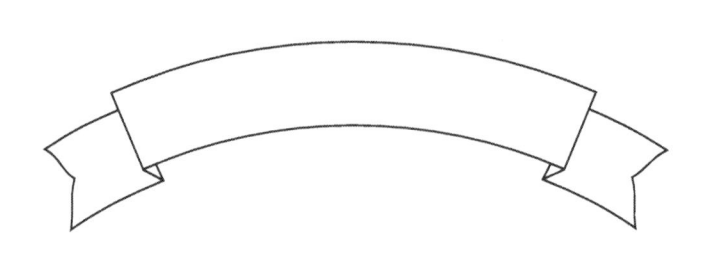

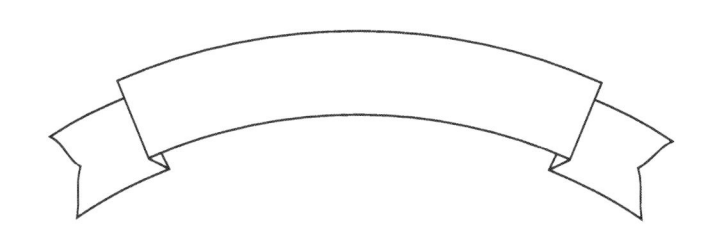

PET CARE Chart

WEEK COMMENCING _____

	TIME	FOOD/WATER	ACCIDENT	WALK	TRAINING
MON					
TUE					
WED					
THUR					
FRI					
SAT					
SUN					

PROGRESS NOTES

PET CARE *Chart*

WEEK COMMENCING _____

	TIME	FOOD/WATER	ACCIDENT	WALK	TRAINING
MON					
TUE					
WED					
THUR					
FRI					
SAT					
SUN					

PROGRESS NOTES

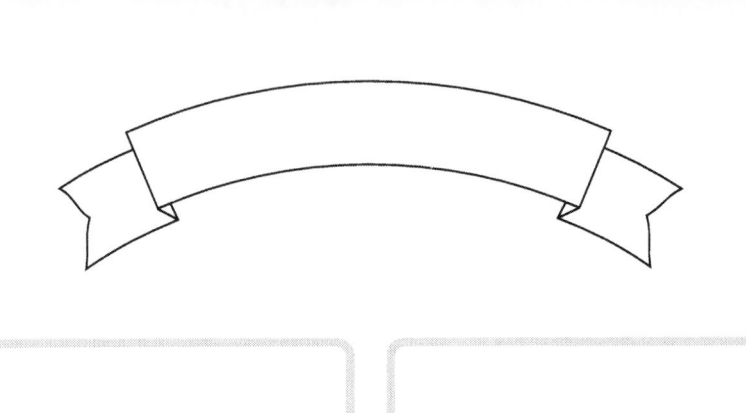

WOOF!

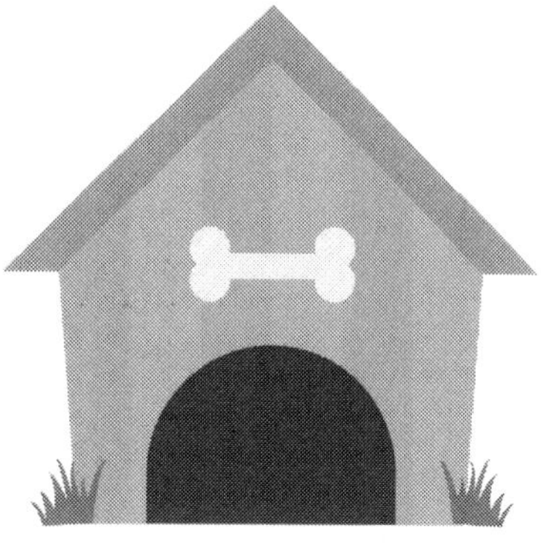

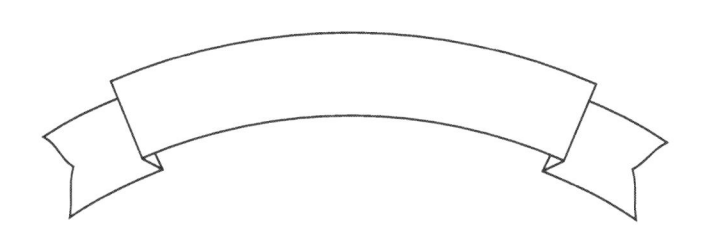

PET CARE *Chart*

WEEK COMMENCING _____

	TIME	FOOD/WATER	ACCIDENT	WALK	TRAINING
MON					
TUE					
WED					
THUR					
FRI					
SAT					
SUN					

PROGRESS NOTES

PET CARE *Chart*

WEEK COMMENCING _____

	TIME	FOOD/WATER	ACCIDENT	WALK	TRAINING
MON					
TUE					
WED					
THUR					
FRI					
SAT					
SUN					

PROGRESS NOTES

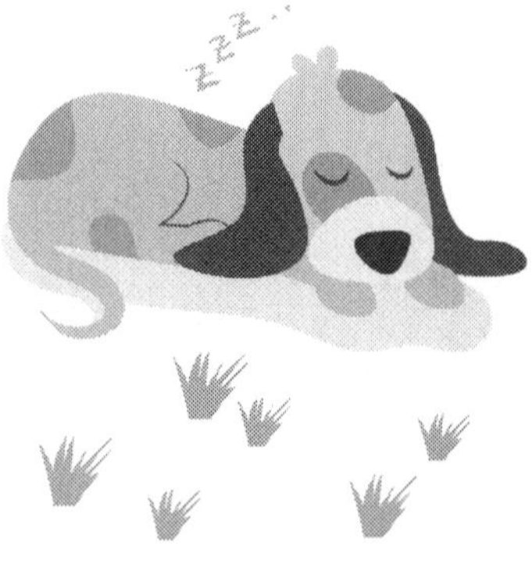

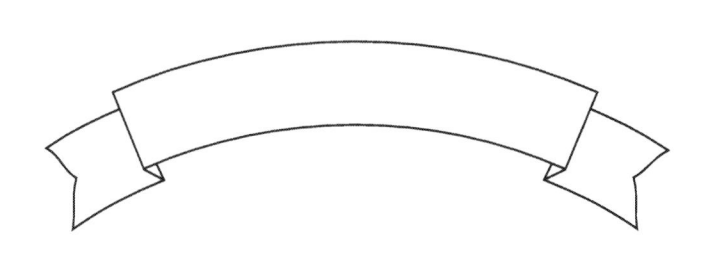

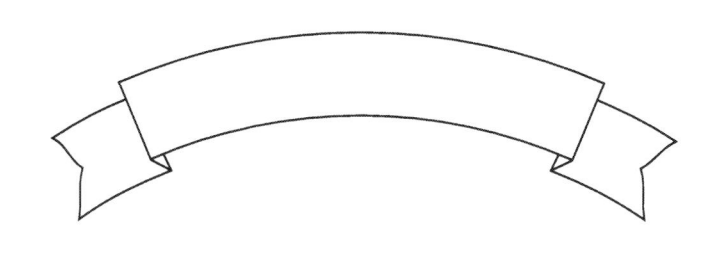

WOOF!

PET CARE *Chart*

WEEK COMMENCING _____

	TIME	FOOD/WATER	ACCIDENT	WALK	TRAINING
MON					
TUE					
WED					
THUR					
FRI					
SAT					
SUN					

PROGRESS NOTES

PET CARE Chart

WEEK COMMENCING _____

	TIME	FOOD/WATER	ACCIDENT	WALK	TRAINING
MON					
TUE					
WED					
THUR					
FRI					
SAT					
SUN					

PROGRESS NOTES

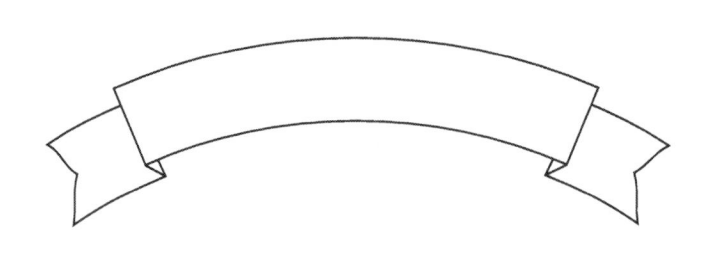

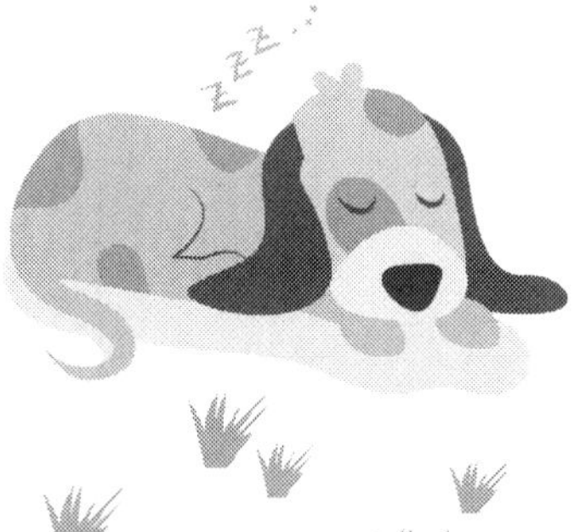

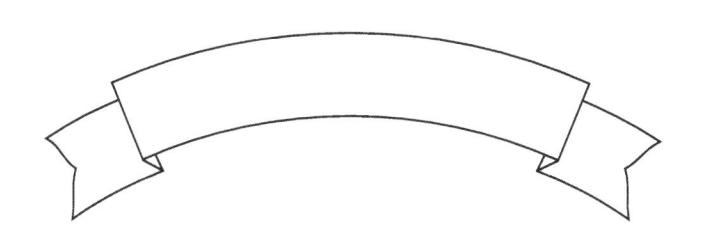

PET CARE *Chart*

WEEK COMMENCING _____

	TIME	FOOD/WATER	ACCIDENT	WALK	TRAINING
MON					
TUE					
WED					
THUR					
FRI					
SAT					
SUN					

PROGRESS NOTES

PET CARE Chart

WEEK COMMENCING _____

	TIME	FOOD/WATER	ACCIDENT	WALK	TRAINING
MON					
TUE					
WED					
THUR					
FRI					
SAT					
SUN					

PROGRESS NOTES

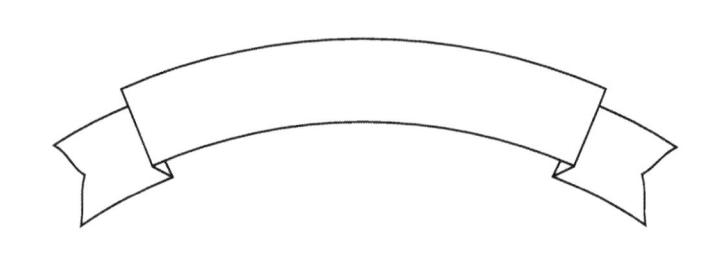

WOOF!

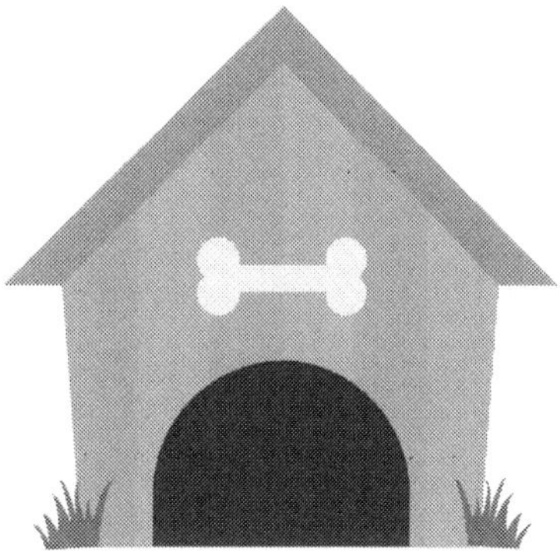

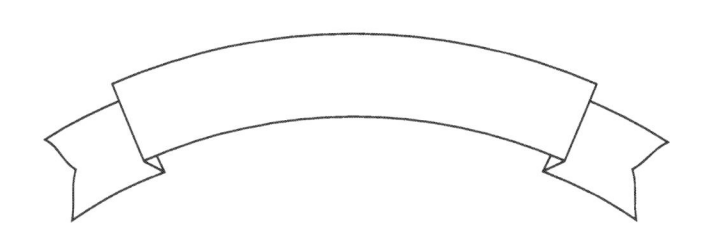

PET CARE *Chart*

WEEK COMMENCING _____

	TIME	FOOD/WATER	ACCIDENT	WALK	TRAINING
MON					
TUE					
WED					
THUR					
FRI					
SAT					
SUN					

PROGRESS NOTES

PET CARE *Chart*

WEEK COMMENCING _____

	TIME	FOOD/WATER	ACCIDENT	WALK	TRAINING
MON					
TUE					
WED					
THUR					
FRI					
SAT					
SUN					

PROGRESS NOTES

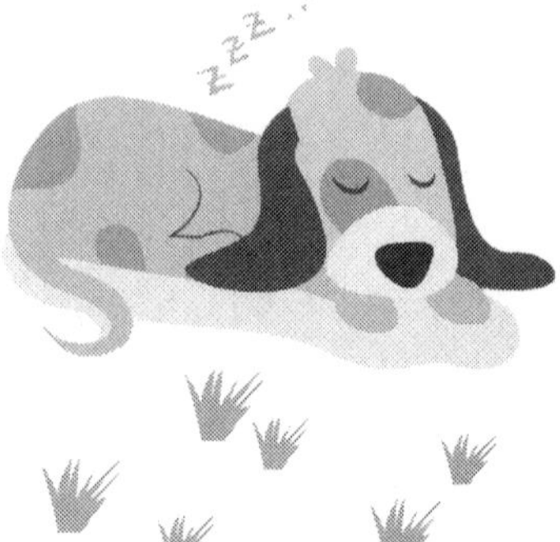

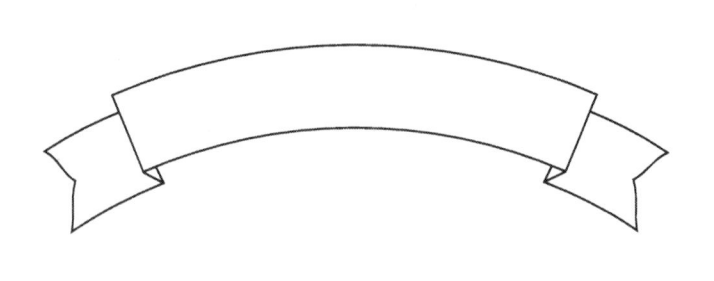

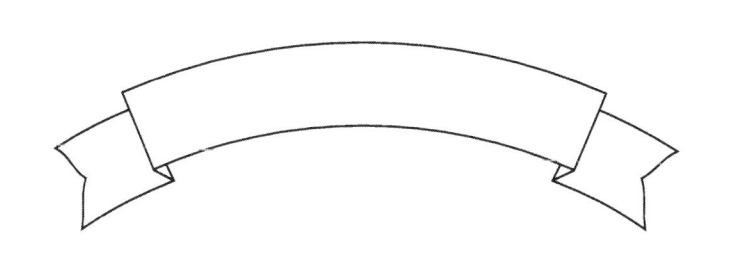

WOOF!

PET CARE Chart

WEEK COMMENCING _____

	TIME	FOOD/WATER	ACCIDENT	WALK	TRAINING
MON					
TUE					
WED					
THUR					
FRI					
SAT					
SUN					

PROGRESS NOTES

PET CARE Chart

WEEK COMMENCING _____

	TIME	FOOD/WATER	ACCIDENT	WALK	TRAINING
MON					
TUE					
WED					
THUR					
FRI					
SAT					
SUN					

PROGRESS NOTES

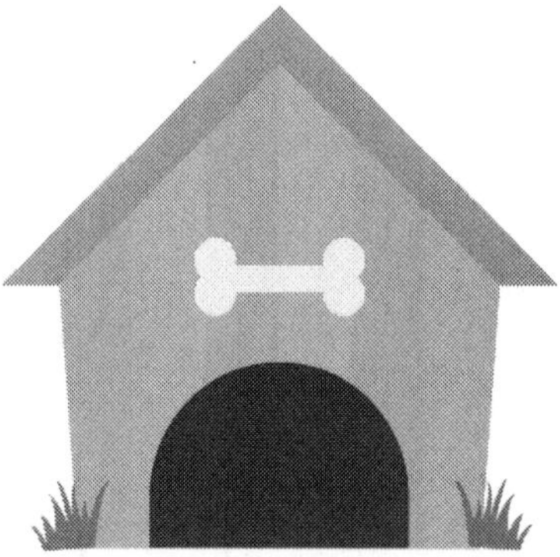

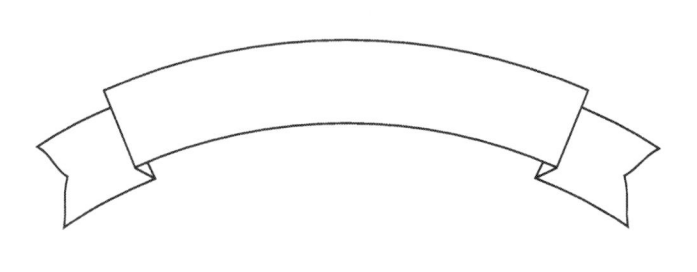

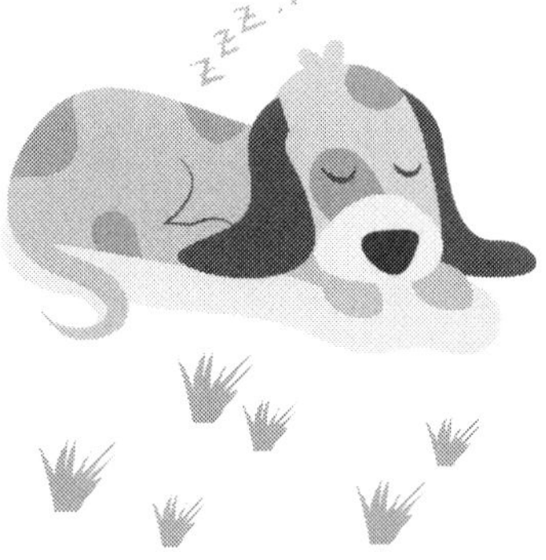

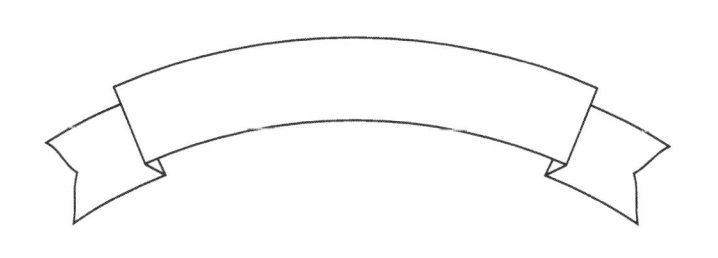

PET CARE Chart

WEEK COMMENCING _____

	TIME	FOOD/WATER	ACCIDENT	WALK	TRAINING
MON					
TUE					
WED					
THUR					
FRI					
SAT					
SUN					

PROGRESS NOTES

PET CARE Chart

WEEK COMMENCING _____

	TIME	FOOD/WATER	ACCIDENT	WALK	TRAINING
MON					
TUE					
WED					
THUR					
FRI					
SAT					
SUN					

PROGRESS NOTES

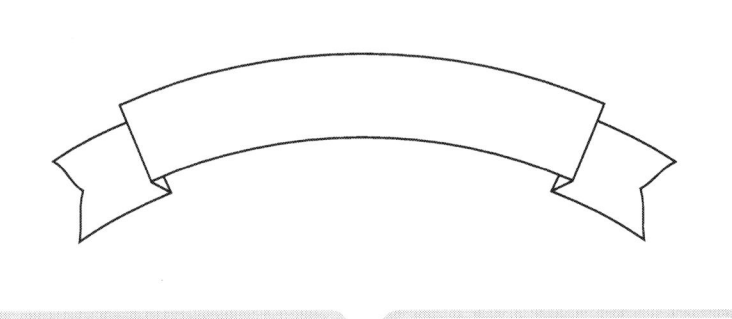

WOOF!

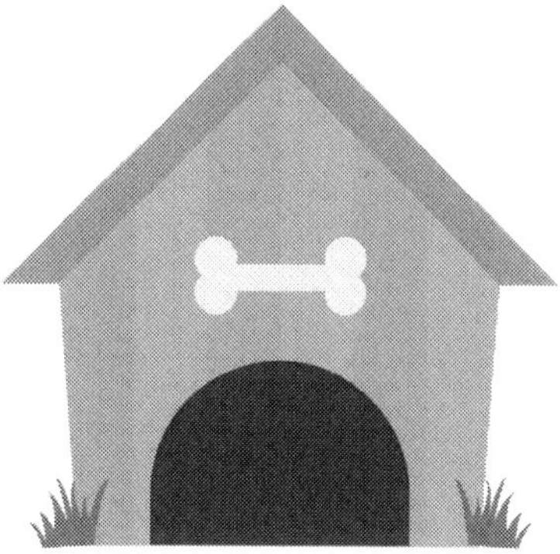

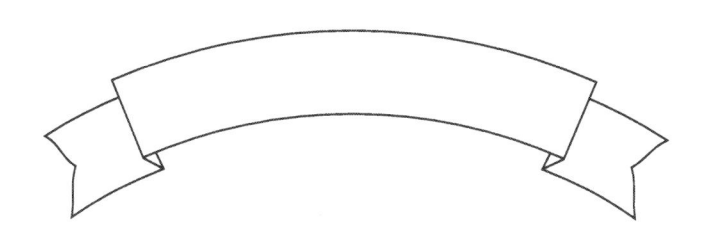

PET CARE Chart

WEEK COMMENCING _____

	TIME	FOOD/WATER	ACCIDENT	WALK	TRAINING
MON					
TUE					
WED					
THUR					
FRI					
SAT					
SUN					

PROGRESS NOTES

PET CARE Chart

WEEK COMMENCING

	TIME	FOOD/WATER	ACCIDENT	WALK	TRAINING
MON					
TUE					
WED					
THUR					
FRI					
SAT					
SUN					

PROGRESS NOTES

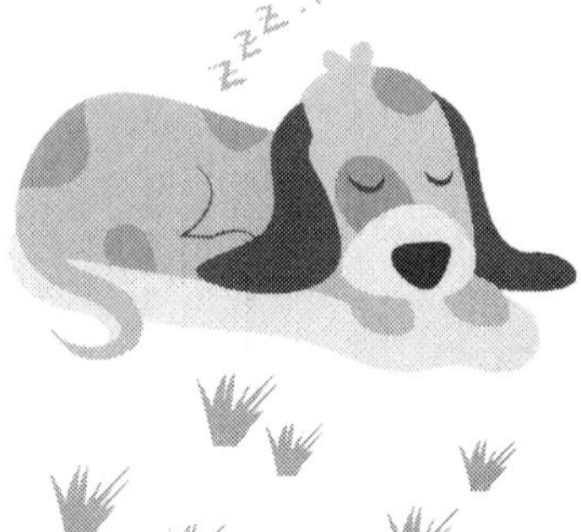

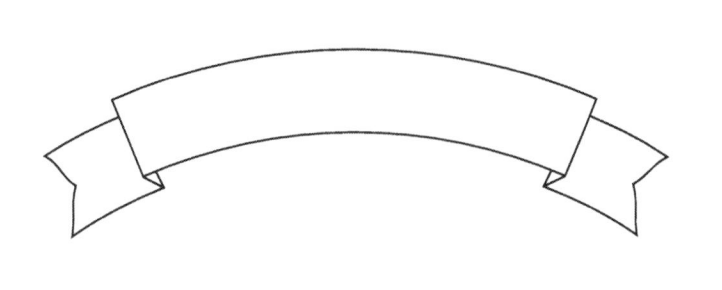

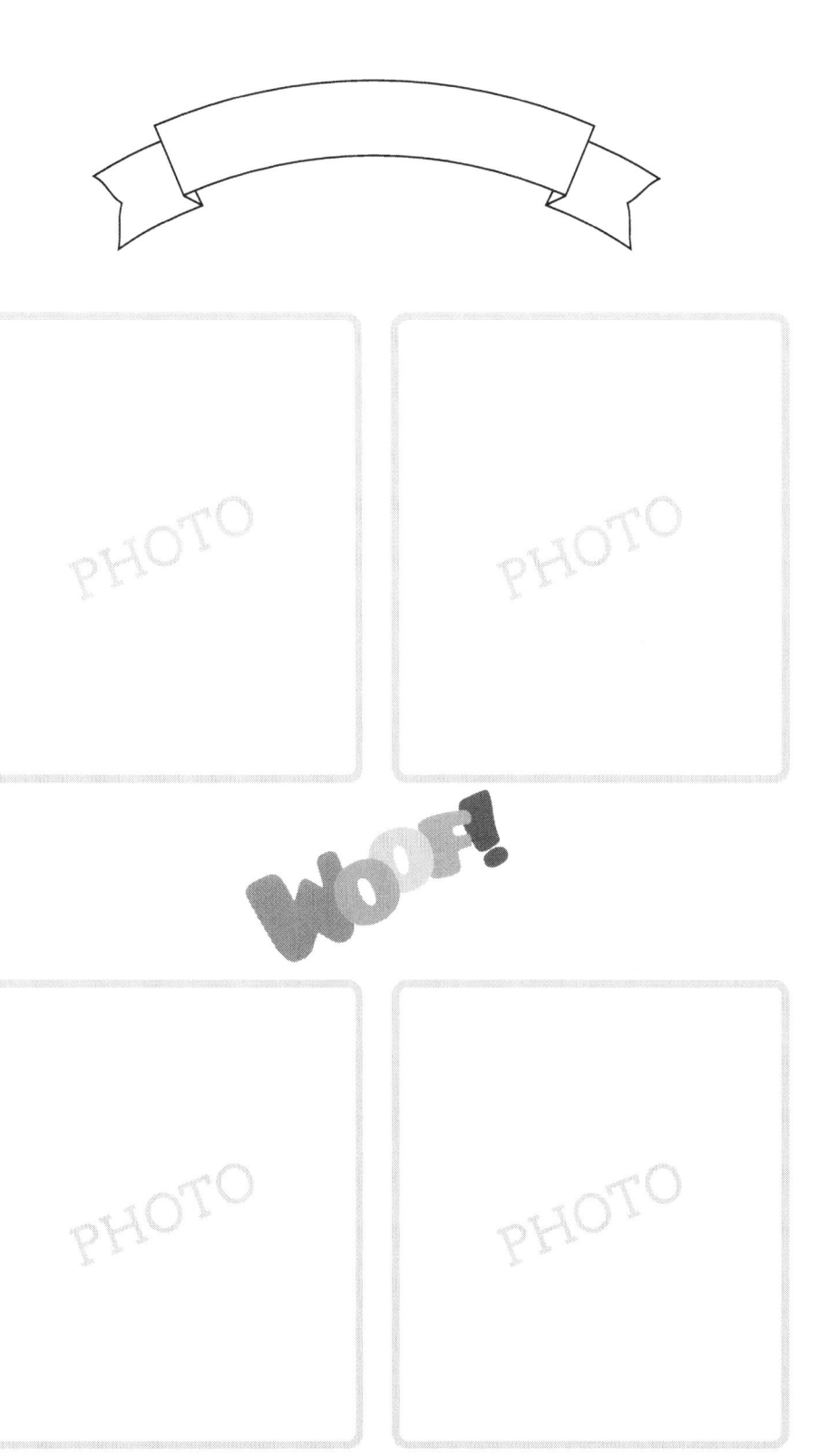

WOOF!

PET CARE Chart

WEEK COMMENCING _____

	TIME	FOOD/WATER	ACCIDENT	WALK	TRAINING
MON					
TUE					
WED					
THUR					
FRI					
SAT					
SUN					

PROGRESS NOTES

PET CARE Chart

WEEK COMMENCING _____

TIME	FOOD/WATER	ACCIDENT	WALK	TRAINING
MON				
TUE				
WED				
THUR				
FRI				
SAT				
SUN				

PROGRESS NOTES

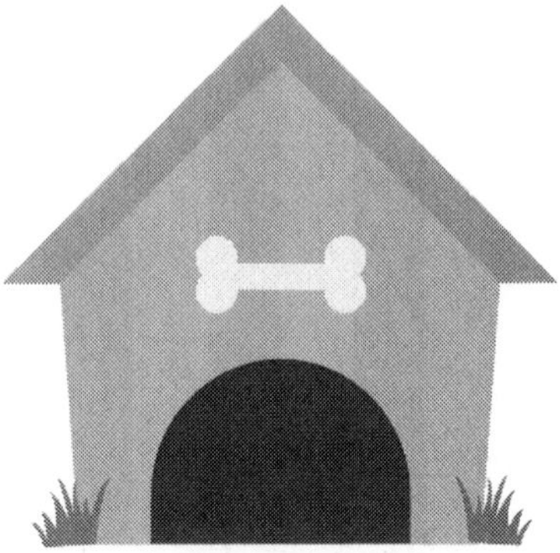

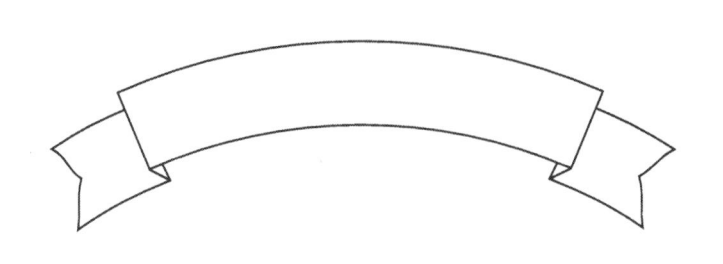

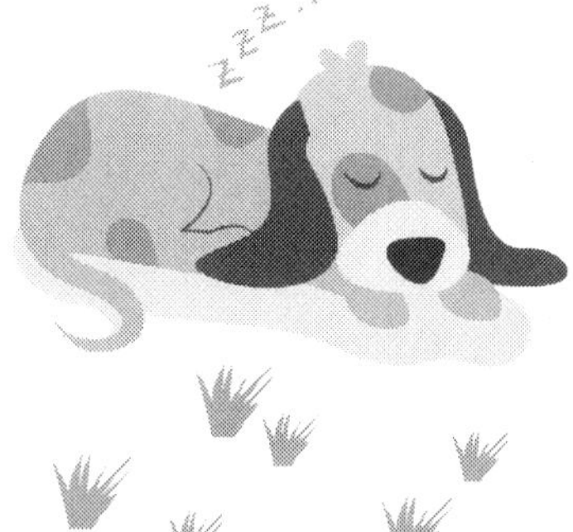

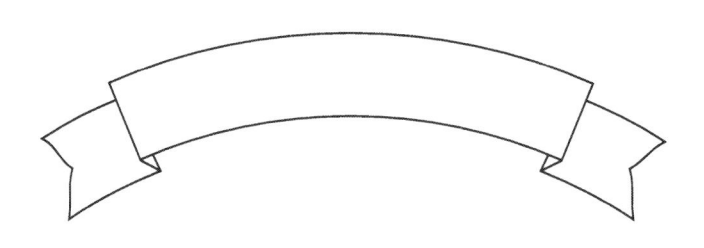

PET CARE Chart

WEEK COMMENCING _____

TIME	FOOD/WATER	ACCIDENT	WALK	TRAINING
MON				
TUE				
WED				
THUR				
FRI				
SAT				
SUN				

PROGRESS NOTES

PET CARE Chart

WEEK COMMENCING _____

	TIME	FOOD/WATER	ACCIDENT	WALK	TRAINING
MON					
TUE					
WED					
THUR					
FRI					
SAT					
SUN					

PROGRESS NOTES

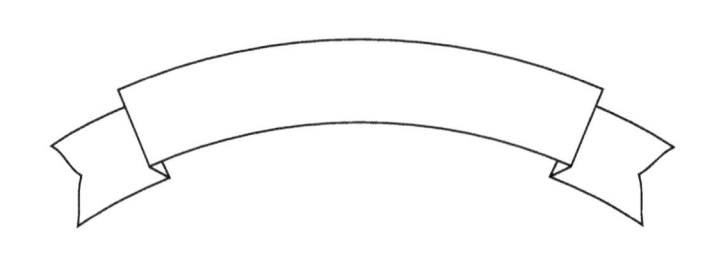

WOOF!

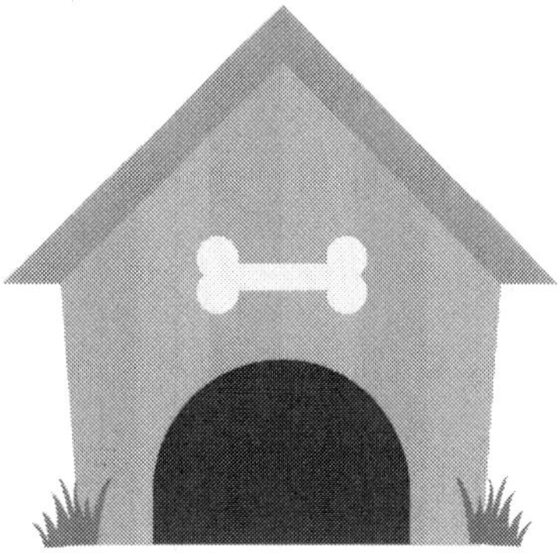

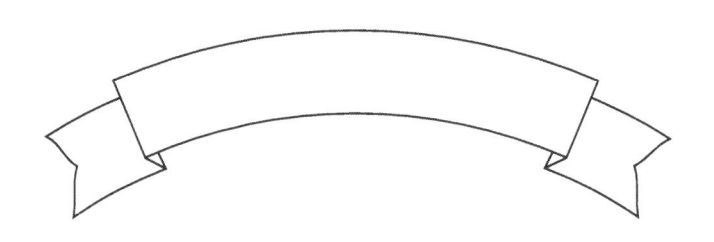

PET CARE Chart

WEEK COMMENCING _____

	TIME	FOOD/WATER	ACCIDENT	WALK	TRAINING
MON					
TUE					
WED					
THUR					
FRI					
SAT					
SUN					

PROGRESS NOTES

1 TODAY

HOW WE CELEBRATED

Printed in Great Britain
by Amazon